Go for Kids: A Beginner's Guide for Kids Aged 6+

By Anthony Colasante

Table of Contents

1. **Welcome to Your Coding Adventure!**
   - What Is Coding?
   - Why Is Coding Fun?
   - How Do Computers Understand Code?
2. **Meet Go the Gopher!**
   - Who Is Go?
   - Setting Up Our Coding Playground
   - Writing Your First Go Program
3. **Talking to the Computer**
   - Saying "Hello, World!"
   - Making the Computer Speak
4. **Numbers and Math Magic**
   - Playing with Numbers
   - Adding, Subtracting, and More
5. **Storing Treasures: Variables**
   - Keeping Secrets in Boxes

- Different Kinds of Boxes (Data Types)
1. **Making Choices: If and Else**
    - Yes or No? Making Decisions
    - Choose Your Own Adventure Stories
1. **Loop-de-Loop: Doing Things Over and Over**
    - Let's Go in Circles with Loops
    - Counting with For Loops
1. **Fantastic Functions**
    - Magic Tricks Called Functions
    - Creating Your Own Functions
1. **Collections of Fun: Arrays and Slices**
    - Keeping Track of Many Things
    - Playing with Lists
1. **Strings: Words and Sentences**
    - Talking in Code
    - Fun with Words and Letters
1. **Go Coding Projects**
    - Making a Simple Game

- Creating a Fun Quiz
- Drawing Shapes with Code

1. **Your Next Steps in Coding**
   - Exploring More with Go
   - Other Fun Coding Languages to Try

Appendix

- Glossary of Coding Terms
- Helpful Resources for Kids
- Answer Key to Exercises

Chapter 1: Welcome to Your Coding Adventure!

What Is Coding?

Hello there, little adventurer! Have you ever played with building blocks or puzzles? Coding is a bit like that, but instead of building towers or solving puzzles with your hands, you use a computer!

Coding is telling a computer what to do by giving it step-by-step instructions. Imagine you're telling a friend how to make a sandwich. You'd tell them each step, right? First, get the bread, then spread the peanut butter, and so on. That's what coding is—giving instructions so the computer knows exactly what you want it to do.

Why Is Coding Fun?

Coding is like magic! Here's why it's so much fun:

- **Create Your Own Games and Stories**: Ever wanted to make your own video game or animated story? With coding, you can bring your ideas to life!
- **Solve Puzzles**: Coding challenges your brain in a fun way. It's like solving a mystery or completing a treasure hunt.
- **Be Creative**: You can make colorful art, funny sounds, and cool animations. The sky's the limit!
-

Share with Friends and Family: Show off your creations and maybe even teach others how to code.

When you code, you're the boss of the computer. How cool is that?

How Do Computers Understand Code?

You might wonder, "How does a computer understand what I'm telling it?" Great question!

Think of the computer as a very smart but super-literal robot. It doesn't understand feelings or guesses—only clear instructions. Computers speak a special language made up of zeros and ones called **binary code**. But don't worry; you don't have to learn that!

Instead, we use programming languages like **Go** (that's the one we'll learn!) to write instructions in a way that's easier for us to understand. The computer then translates our Go code into binary so it can follow our instructions.

Imagine you have a friend who speaks another language. You might use a translator to talk to each other. In the same way, programming languages help us talk to computers.

Are you excited to start coding? Grab your imagination, and let's jump into the world of Go with our friend, Go the Gopher!

Chapter 2: Meet Go the Gopher!

Who Is Go?

Hello again, young coder! Are you ready to meet a new friend? Let me introduce you to **Go the Gopher**!

Go the Gopher is the fun and friendly mascot of the **Go programming language**. Just like how Mickey Mouse represents Disney, Go the Gopher represents the Go language. Go is a programming language created by some smart people at Google to make coding easier and more fun!

Why is Go special?

- **Easy to Learn**: Go is simple and straightforward, making it great for beginners like you.
- **Fast and Powerful**: Even though it's easy, Go is used to build big, important programs all over the world.
- **Fun Mascot**: Who doesn't love a cute gopher friend to help them learn?

Are you excited to start coding with Go the Gopher? Let's set up our coding playground!

Setting Up Our Coding Playground

Before we start our adventure, we need a place to write and run our Go code. Think of it like setting up your art station before painting a masterpiece!

Option 1: Using an Online Go Playground

The easiest way to start is by using the **Go Playground**, a website where you can write and run Go code without installing anything.

Steps:

1. **Open Your Web Browser**: This could be Chrome, Firefox, Safari, or any other browser.
2. **Go to the Go Playground**: Type play.golang.org in the address bar and press Enter.
3. **You're Ready!**: You'll see a page with some code already written. That's your coding playground!

Option 2: Installing Go on Your Computer

If you want to be a super coder, you can install Go on your computer. You might need an adult's help for this part.

Steps for Windows:

1. **Download Go:**
    - Visit golang.org/dl.
    - Click on the link that says **"Go for Windows"**.
1. **Install Go:**
    - Open the file you downloaded (it ends with .msi).
    - Follow the instructions by clicking "Next" until it's done.

Steps for Mac:

1. **Download Go:**
    - Visit golang.org/dl.
    - Click on the link that says **"Go for macOS"**.
1. **Install Go:**
    - Open the file you downloaded (it ends with .pkg).
    - Follow the instructions by clicking "Continue" until it's done.

Steps for Linux:

-

Installing Go on Linux can be a bit tricky. It's best to use the online Go Playground or ask an adult for help.

Choosing a Code Editor

A code editor is like a special notebook where we write our code.

- **Beginner Option**: Use a simple text editor like **Notepad** (Windows) or **TextEdit** (Mac).
- **Advanced Option**: Install a free code editor like **Visual Studio Code**.

But for now, the **Go Playground** is perfect!

Writing Your First Go Program

Yay! Now that we have our playground ready, let's write our very first Go program. We'll make the computer say hello to us!

Step 1: Open the Go Playground

Go to play.golang.org if you're not there already.

Step 2: Understanding the Starter Code

You might see some code already written:

```go
package main
import "fmt"
func main() {
        fmt.Println("Hello, 世界")
}
```

Let's see what this means:

-

- **package main**: This tells the computer that this is where our program starts.
- **import "fmt"**: We're bringing in some helpers that allow us to print messages.
- **func main() { ... }**: This is the main function where we write what we want the computer to do.
- **fmt.Println("Hello, 世界")**: This line tells the computer to print the message inside the quotes.

Step 3: Changing the Message

Let's make the computer say "Hello, Go Gopher!"

Find the line:
```go
fmt.Println("Hello, 世界")
```

1.

Change it to:
```go
fmt.Println("Hello, Go Gopher!")
```

1.

Now your code should look like this:

```go
package main
import "fmt"
func main() {
        fmt.Println("Hello, Go Gopher!")
```

}

Step 4: Running Your Code

1. **Click the "Run" Button**: It's a big blue button at the top.

See the Output: Below the code, you should see:

Hello, Go Gopher!

1.

Congratulations! You've just written and run your first Go program!

Step 5: Experimenting

Try changing the message to your own name or any greeting you like.

Example:

go
fmt.Println("Hi, I'm a Go programmer!")

What Did We Learn?

- **Printing Messages**: We used fmt.Println to tell the computer to print a message.

- **Running Code**: We learned how to run our code and see the output.

Tip: If you ever get stuck, don't worry. Even the best programmers make mistakes. Just check your code and try again.

Are you ready to explore more? In the next chapter, we'll learn how to make the computer talk to us by asking questions and getting answers. Let's keep coding with Go the Gopher!

Chapter 3: Talking to the Computer

Saying "Hello, World!"

Welcome back, junior coder! Now that we've set up our coding playground, it's time to start talking to the computer. Let's begin by making it say "Hello, World!" This is a traditional first step for programmers all around the world. Ready? Let's go!

Step 1: Open Your Coding Playground

- **Using the Go Playground**: Go to play.golang.org.

- **Using Your Text Editor**: Open the text editor you chose earlier.

Step 2: Write Your Code

Type the following code exactly as you see it:

```go
package main
import "fmt"
func main() {
    fmt.Println("Hello, World!")
}
```

Let's understand what this means:

-

- **package main**: This tells Go that this is the main package where our program starts.
- **import "fmt"**: We are bringing in a helper package named fmt that allows us to print messages.
- **func main() { ... }**: This is the main function where all the action happens.
- **fmt.Println("Hello, World!")**: This line tells the computer to print "Hello, World!" on the screen.

Step 3: Run Your Code

- **In the Go Playground**:
  - Click the **"Run"** button at the top of the page.
- **On Your Computer**:
  - Save your file as hello.go.
  - Open your command prompt or terminal.
  - Navigate to the folder where you saved your file.
  - Type go run hello.go and press Enter.

Step 4: See the Output

You should see:

Hello, World!

Hooray! You've just written your first Go program that talks to you!

Experiment Time!

Try changing the message inside the quotation marks to something else.

Example:

```go
fmt.Println("Hello, [Your Name]!")
```

Replace [Your Name] with your actual name.

Run It Again

After making changes, run your program again to see the new message.

Making the Computer Speak

Now that we've made the computer say "Hello," let's make it say more things. We can add more lines to make a conversation.

Adding More Messages

Let's expand our program:

```go
package main
import "fmt"
func main() {
    fmt.Println("Hello, World!")
    fmt.Println("My name is Go the Gopher.")
    fmt.Println("What's your name?")
    fmt.Println("Nice to meet you!")
```

}

Understanding the Code

- Each fmt.Println line prints a new message.

- The computer will display these messages one after the other.

Run Your Program

Run your program again to see the conversation:

```vbnet
Hello, World!
My name is Go the Gopher.
What's your name?
Nice to meet you!
```

Let's Make It Even Better!

Add more lines to make the computer say whatever you like.

Example:

```go
package main
import "fmt"
func main() {
    fmt.Println("Hello!")
    fmt.Println("Do you like coding?")
    fmt.Println("Coding is so much fun!")
    fmt.Println(' Let's create amazing things together.")
}
```

Run It Again

Run your program to see the new messages.

What Did We Learn?

- **Printing Multiple Messages**: By adding more fmt.Println lines, we can make the computer say more things.
- **Order Matters**: The computer prints the messages in the order they appear in the code.
- **Creativity**: You can make the computer say anything you like (as long as it's appropriate and kind).

Tips for Young Coders:

- **Quotation Marks**: Always put your messages inside "quotation marks" so the computer knows it's text.
- **Parentheses and Brackets**: Make sure to include all the necessary () and {} symbols.
- **Have Fun**: Experiment with different messages and see what happens!

Challenge Yourself!

- **Create a Joke**: Make the computer tell a funny joke.

Write a Poem: Use multiple fmt.Println lines to write a short poem.
-

Ask Questions: Have the computer ask you questions (even if it can't hear your answers yet!).

Great job! You've learned how to make the computer speak by printing messages. In the next chapter, we'll dive into **Numbers and Math Magic**, where we'll play with numbers and see how Go can help us with math. Keep up the fantastic work, little programmer!

Chapter 4: Numbers and Math Magic

Playing with Numbers

Hello, young explorer! Are you ready to dive into the magical world of numbers with Go the Gopher? Just like you count your toys or share candies with friends, computers can play with numbers too! Let's find out how.

Numbers in Go

In Go, we use numbers just like we do in real life. There are two main types of numbers:

- **Whole Numbers**: Like 1, 2, 10, or 100 (also called integers).
- **Decimal Numbers**: Like 1.5, 2.75, or 3.14 (also called floating-point numbers).

For now, we'll start with whole numbers.

Let's Try Printing Numbers

First, let's make the computer show us some numbers. Open your Go Playground or coding editor, and let's write some code!

```go
package main
import "fmt"
func main() {
```

```
    fmt.Println("Let's play with numbers'")
    fmt.Println(7)
    fmt.Println(42)
    fmt.Println(100)
}
```

When you run this code, the computer will print:

```vbnet
Let's play with numbers!
7
42
100
```

Your Turn!

- **Change the Numbers**: Try changing the numbers to your favorite numbers.
- **Add More Numbers**: Add more fmt.Println lines to print more numbers.

Combining Text and Numbers

We can also print text and numbers together!

```go
package main
import "fmt"
func main() {
    fmt.Println("I have", 5, "books.")
}
```

Output:

```css
I have 5 books.
```

Adding, Subtracting, and More

Now, let's make the computer do some math for us! We'll learn how to add, subtract, multiply, and divide numbers.

Adding Numbers

Adding is like putting things together.

```go
package main
import "fmt"
func main() {
   fmt.Println("Addition:")
   fmt.Println(2 + 3)
}
```

Output:

```
makefile
Addition:
5
```

The computer added 2 and 3 and got 5!

Subtracting Numbers

Subtracting is like taking things away.

```go
package main
import "fmt"
func main() {
   fmt.Println("Subtraction:")
   fmt.Println(10 - 4)
}
```

Output:

```makefile
Subtraction:
6
```

Multiplying Numbers ✖

Multiplying is like adding the same number many times.

```go
package main
import "fmt"
func main() {
    fmt.Println("Multiplication:")
    fmt.Println(3 * 4)
}
```

Output:

```makefile
Multiplication:
12
```

Dividing Numbers

Dividing is like sharing equally.

```go
package main
import "fmt"
func main() {
    fmt.Println("Division:")
    fmt.Println(20 / 5)
}
```

Output:

```makefile
Division:
```

4

Mixing It Up!

We can even combine different operations.

```go
package main
import "fmt"
func main() {
   fmt.Println("Mixed Operations:")
   fmt.Println((2 + 3) * 4)
}
```

Output:

```yaml
Mixed Operations:
20
```

Parentheses Matter!

Just like in math class, parentheses () tell the computer which calculations to do first.

Fun Math Examples

Example 1: Counting Apples

```go
package main
import "fmt"
func main() {
   fmt.Println("I have", 3, "apples.")
   fmt.Println("My friend gives me", 2, "more apples.")
   fmt.Println("Now I have", 3 + 2, "apples!")
}
```

Output:

mathematica
I have 3 apples.
My friend gives me 2 more apples.
Now I have 5 apples!

Example 2: Sharing Cookies

```go
package main
import "fmt"
func main() {
    fmt.Println("We have", 12, "cookies.")
    fmt.Println("We share them among", 4, "friends.")
    fmt.Println("Each friend gets", 12 / 4, "cookies.")
}
```

Output:

vbnet
We have 12 cookies.
We share them among 4 friends.
Each friend gets 3 cookies.

Example 3: Toy Cars

```go
package main
import "fmt"
func main() {
    fmt.Println("I have", 5, "toy cars.")
    fmt.Println("I lost", 2, "cars.")
    fmt.Println("Now I have", 5 - 2, "cars left.")
}
```

Output:

css

I have 5 toy cars.
I lost 2 cars.
Now I have 3 cars left.

Try It Yourself!

- **Create Your Own Story**: Write a small story using numbers, like counting balloons or sharing candies.
- **Experiment with Math**: Try different math operations with different numbers.

Example:

```go
package main
import "fmt"
func main() {
    fmt.Println("There are", 6, "birds on a tree.")
    fmt.Println("3 more birds join them.")
    fmt.Println("Now there are", 6 + 3, "birds on the tree.")
}
```

What Did We Learn?

- **Numbers in Go**: How to use numbers in your programs.
- **Math Operations**: Adding +, subtracting -, multiplying *, and dividing /.
- **Combining Text and Numbers**: Printing messages that include numbers.
-

Order of Operations: Using parentheses () to control the order of calculations.

Tips for Success:

- **Check Your Math**: Make sure your calculations are correct.
- **Use Spaces**: Adding spaces in your print statements makes the output look nice.
- **Have Fun**: Be creative and make up your own math adventures!

Challenge Time!

1. **Birthday Countdown**: If it's 10 days until your birthday, write a program that counts down the days.

Animal Legs: If you have 3 cats and each cat has 4 legs, how many legs are there in total?
go

```
fmt.Println("Total legs:", 3 * 4)
```

1.

Pocket Money: If you have $10 and you buy a toy that costs $4, how much money do you have left?
go

```
fmt.Println("Money left:", 10 - 4)
```

1.

Great job, superstar coder! ☐ You've mastered numbers and math in Go. Numbers help us solve problems and create fun programs. Keep practicing, and in the next chapter, we'll learn how to **Store Treasures: Variables**. Get ready to discover how to keep your numbers and words safe in special boxes!

Chapter 5: Storing Treasures: Variables

Keeping Secrets in Boxes

Hello, young coder! Have you ever had a special box where you keep your favorite toys, stickers, or secret notes? In programming, we have something similar called **variables**. Variables are like boxes where we can store information—like numbers, words, or other data—so we can use them later in our programs.

Imagine you have a box labeled "Favorite Toy," and inside it, you place your toy car. Whenever you want to play with your toy car, you know exactly where to find it! Variables work the same way: we give them names so we can easily access the data stored inside.

What Is a Variable?

A **variable** is a named container that holds a value. This value can change, which is why it's called a "variable"—it can vary!

Let's Try It!

Let's write some Go code to see variables in action.

```go
package main

import "fmt"

func main() {
    var favoriteNumber int = 7
```

fmt.Println("My favorite number is", favoriteNumber)

}

What's Happening Here?

- var favoriteNumber int = 7: We're creating a variable named favoriteNumber that holds an integer (int) value of 7.

- fmt.Println("My favorite number is", favoriteNumber): We're printing a message that includes the value stored in favoriteNumber.

Run the Code

When you run this code, you'll see:

csharp

My favorite number is 7

Isn't that cool? You've stored a number in a variable and used it in your program!

Different Kinds of Boxes (Data Types)

Just like you might have different boxes for toys, books, or snacks, variables can store different kinds of data. These are called **data types**.

Common Data Types in Go

1. **int**: Used for whole numbers (like 1, 2, 100).
2. **float64**: Used for numbers with decimals (like 3.14, 2.5).

3. **string**: Used for text (like "Hello" or "Go Gopher").
4. **bool**: Used for true or false values.

Examples of Different Data Types

Storing a Whole Number

go

```
package main

import "fmt"

func main() {
    var age int = 10
    fmt.Println("I am", age, "years old.")
}
```

Output:

css

I am 10 years old.

Storing a Decimal Number

go

```
package main

import "fmt"

func main() {
    var pi float64 = 3.14
    fmt.Println("The value of pi is", pi)
```

}

Output:

csharp

The value of pi is 3.14

Storing Text

go

```go
package main

import "fmt"

func main() {
    var name string = "Alex"
    fmt.Println("Hello, my name is", name)
}
```

Output:

csharp

Hello, my name is Alex

Storing True or False

go

```go
package main

import "fmt"

func main() {
```

```go
var isSunny bool = true
fmt.Println("Is it sunny today?", isSunny)
}
```

Output:

vbnet

Is it sunny today? true

A Shorter Way to Create Variables

Go allows us to create variables in a shorter way using :=.

```go
package main

import "fmt"

func main() {
    favoriteColor := "blue"
    fmt.Println("My favorite color is", favoriteColor)
}
```

This is the same as writing:

```go
var favoriteColor string = "blue"
```

Changing What's Inside the Box

Variables can change over time. Let's see how we can update a variable.

go
```
package main
import "fmt"
func main() {
    var score int = 0
    fmt.Println("Starting score:", score)
    score = 10
    fmt.Println("Updated score:", score)
}
```

Output:

```yaml
Starting score: 0
Updated score: 10
```

We started with a score of 0 and then changed it to 10.

Using Variables Together

We can use variables in calculations or combine them in messages.

go
```
package main
import "fmt"
func main() {
```

```
apples := 4

bananas := 3

totalFruits := apples + bananas

fmt.Println("Total fruits:", totalFruits)

}
```

Output:

mathematica

Total fruits: 7

Variable Naming Rules

- **Start with a letter**: Variable names should begin with a letter (a–z or A–Z).
- **Letters and numbers**: After the first letter, you can use letters and numbers.
- **No spaces or special characters**: Don't use spaces or symbols like !, @, #, etc.
- **Case-sensitive**: age and Age are considered different variables.

Tips for Good Variable Names

- **Make it meaningful**: Name your variables so that they describe what's inside.
- **Keep it simple**: Short names are easier to read and type.

Good examples:

- age
- totalScore
- isGameOver

Bad examples:

- a (too short and unclear)
- 1stPlace (starts with a number)
- my age (contains a space)

Practice Time!

Let's practice creating variables.

Example 1: Favorite Animal

```go
package main

import "fmt"

func main() {
    favoriteAnimal := "dolphin"
    fmt.Println("My favorite animal is the", favoriteAnimal)
```

}

Output:

csharp

My favorite animal is the dolphin

Example 2: Simple Math

go

package main

import "fmt"

func main() {

   numberOne := 5

   numberTwo := 10

   sum := numberOne + numberTwo

   fmt.Println("The sum is", sum)

}

Output:

python

The sum is 15

Example 3: True or False

go

package main

```go
import "fmt"
func main() {
    isRaining := false
    fmt.Println("Is it raining today?", isRaining)
}
```

Output:

vbnet

Is it raining today? false

What Did We Learn?

- **Variables are like boxes**: They store data we can use later.
- **Different data types**: int, float64, string, and bool.
- **Creating variables**: Using var name type = value or name := value.
- **Updating variables**: We can change the value stored in a variable.
- **Using variables**: In calculations and to build messages.

Challenge Time!

Story Time: Create variables to tell a short story.
go

```go
package main

import "fmt"

func main() {
    characterName := "Lily"

    characterAge := 8

    favoriteHobby := "painting"

    fmt.Println("Once upon a time, there was a child named", characterName)

    fmt.Println("They were", characterAge, "years old and loved", favoriteHobby)

}
```

Output:

css

Once upon a time, there was a child named Lily

They were 8 years old and loved painting

1.

Temperature Check: Store today's temperature and print a message.

go

```go
package main

import "fmt"

func main() {
```

```go
    temperature := 25.5

    fmt.Println("Today's temperature is", temperature, "degrees Celsius.")
}
```

Output:
mathematica

Today's temperature is 25.5 degrees Celsius.

1. **Basketball Game**: Keep track of points scored.

go

```go
package main

import "fmt"

func main() {
    teamScore := 0

    fmt.Println("Team score:", teamScore)

    teamScore = teamScore + 2

    fmt.Println("Team scored a basket!")

    fmt.Println("Team score:", teamScore)
}
```

Output:
yaml

Team score: 0

Team scored a basket!

Team score: 2

1.

Fantastic job! You've learned how to store treasures in variables and use different kinds of boxes to keep your data organized. Variables are like the building blocks of programming—they help us remember and use information throughout our programs.

In the next chapter, we'll learn about **Making Choices: If and Else**, where our programs can make decisions based on certain conditions. Get ready to make your code even smarter!

Chapter 6: Making Choices: If and Else

Yes or No? Making Decisions

Hello again, junior programmer! Have you ever played a game where you had to make choices, like deciding whether to turn left or right in a maze? In programming, we can make our programs make choices too! This is done using something called **conditional statements**, or more simply, **if** and **else**.

What Is an If Statement?

An **if statement** lets your program ask a question and decide what to do based on the answer.

Imagine:

- **If** it's raining, **then** take an umbrella.
- **If** you are hungry, **then** eat a snack.

In code, we use if to make these decisions.

Let's Try It!

Let's write a simple program that uses if.

go

package main

import "fmt"

```
func main() {
    age := 7
    if age >= 6 {
        fmt.Println("You are old enough to play this game!")
    }
}
```

What's Happening Here?

- We have a variable age set to 7.
- The if statement checks if age is greater than or equal to 6.
- If the condition is true, the program prints "You are old enough to play this game!"

Run the Code

When you run this code, you'll see:

kotlin

You are old enough to play this game!

Changing the Condition

Try changing the age to 5:

go

age := 5

Run the code again. This time, nothing happens! Why?

Because the condition age >= 6 is not true when age is 5. The program skips the fmt.Println line.

Adding an Else Statement

What if we want the program to say something else when the condition is not true? We can use else.

go

```
package main

import "fmt"

func main() {
    age := 5
    if age >= 6 {
        fmt.Println("You are old enough to play this game!")
    } else {
        fmt.Println("Sorry, you are too young to play this game.")
    }
}
```

Now, when you run the code, you'll see:

kotlin

Sorry, you are too young to play this game.

How Does If and Else Work?

- The if statement checks a condition.

- If the condition is **true**, the code inside the if block runs.

- If the condition is **false**, and there's an else block, the code inside the else block runs.

Using Comparison Operators

In our condition, we used >=, but there are other comparison operators:

- == : equal to
- != : not equal to
- \> : greater than
- < : less than
- \>= : greater than or equal to
- <= : less than or equal to

Examples:

Checking Equality

```go
number := 10
if number == 10 {
    fmt.Println("The number is ten!")
```

}

Checking If Not Equal

```go
color := "red"
if color != "blue" {
    fmt.Println("The color is not blue.")
}
```

Choose Your Own Adventure Stories

Now, let's make something fun! We're going to create a mini "Choose Your Own Adventure" story where the program makes decisions based on choices.

Setting Up the Story

Imagine a story where you can choose to go through a **door** or a **window**.

Let's Code It!

```go
package main

import "fmt"

func main() {
    choice := "door"
    if choice == "door" {
```

```
    fmt.Println("You opened the door and found a treasure chest!")
  } else if choice == "window" {
    fmt.Println("You climbed through the window and found a secret garden!")
  } else {
    fmt.Println("You stayed where you were and missed the adventure.")
  }
}
```

What's Happening Here?

- We have a variable choice set to "door".
- The program checks:
  - **If** choice is "door", it prints about the treasure chest.
  - **Else if** choice is "window", it prints about the secret garden.
  - **Else**, it prints that you missed the adventure.

Run the Code

You should see:

css

You opened the door and found a treasure chest!

Changing Choices

Try changing choice to "window":

go

choice := "window"

Run the code again. Now you'll see:

css

You climbed through the window and found a secret garden!

What if you change choice to "stay"?

go

choice := "stay"

Now the output is:

bash

You stayed where you were and missed the adventure.

Adding User Input (Advanced)

To make the story interactive, we can ask the user for input. This requires using fmt.Scanln, which might be a bit advanced, but let's try it!

go

package main

import "fmt"

func main() {

```
var choice string

fmt.Println("You're standing in front of a house. Do you enter through the 'door' or the 'window'?")

fmt.Scanln(&choice)

if choice == "door" {

    fmt.Println("You opened the door and found a treasure chest!")

} else if choice == "window" {

    fmt.Println("You climbed through the window and found a secret garden!")

} else {

    fmt.Println("You stayed where you were and missed the adventure.")

}
}
```

What's New Here?

- var choice string: We declare a variable choice to store user input.

- fmt.Scanln(&choice): This line waits for the user to type something and press Enter. The input is stored in choice.

Run the Code

The program will ask:
python

You're standing in front of a house. Do you enter through the 'door' or the 'window'?

-
-
  You can type door or window and press Enter.
-

  The program will respond based on your choice.

Note for Go Playground Users

Unfortunately, the Go Playground doesn't support interactive input (fmt.Scanln). To try this code, you need to run it on your computer. Ask an adult to help you set up Go on your machine.

Nested If Statements

We can make our story more complex by adding choices within choices.

go

package main

import "fmt"

func main() {

   var choice string

   fmt.Println("You're in a dark forest. Do you go 'left' or 'right'?")

   fmt.Scanln(&choice)

   if choice == "left" {

```
        fmt.Println("You see a river. Do you 'swim' or 'build' a boat?")
        fmt.Scanln(&choice)
        if choice == "swim" {
            fmt.Println("You swim across safely!")
        } else if choice == "build" {
            fmt.Println("You build a boat and sail across!")
        } else {
            fmt.Println("You wait too long and it's getting dark.")
        }
    } else if choice == "right" {
        fmt.Println("You find a mountain. Do you 'climb' or 'go around'?")
        fmt.Scanln(&choice)
        if choice == "climb" {
            fmt.Println("You reach the top and see a beautiful view!")
        } else if choice == "go around" {
            fmt.Println("You find a hidden valley full of flowers!")
        } else {
            fmt.Println("You decide to camp for the night.")
        }
```

```
} else {
    fmt.Println("You stand still and nothing happens.")
}
}
```

This code is more complex and allows for multiple choices.

Understanding Nested If Statements

- **Nested If**: An if statement inside another if statement.
- It allows the program to make decisions based on previous choices.

Practice Time!

Create Your Own Adventure

Try to create your own story with choices.

Example Outline:

1. Ask the user to choose between "forest" or "beach".
2. If "forest":
   - Choose between "explore" or "rest".
   - If "explore": something happens.
   - If "rest": something else happens.
1. If "beach":
   - Choose between "swim" or "build sandcastle".
   -

If "swim": something happens.
○

If "build sandcastle": something else happens.

Use if, else if, and else statements to build your story.

What Did We Learn?

- **If Statements**: How to make decisions in code using if.
- **Else and Else If**: Providing alternative actions when the if condition is false.
- **Comparison Operators**: Using ==, !=, >, <, >=, <= to compare values.
- **Nested If Statements**: Placing an if inside another if to create multiple layers of decision-making.
- **Building Interactive Stories**: Using if statements to create "Choose Your Own Adventure" stories.

Tips for Success:

- **Be Careful with Conditions**: Make sure your if statements have the correct conditions.
- **Use Clear Variable Names**: This makes your code easier to read.
-

Plan Your Story: Before coding, write down the choices and outcomes.

Challenge Time!

Guess the Number Game:
Write a program where the user has to guess a number between 1 and 5.

```go
package main

import "fmt"

func main() {
    var guess int
    secretNumber := 3
    fmt.Println("Guess the secret number between 1 and 5:")
    fmt.Scanln(&guess)
    if guess == secretNumber {
        fmt.Println("You guessed it!")
    } else {
        fmt.Println("Try again!")
    }
}
```

1.

Weather Suggestion:
Ask the user for the weather ("sunny", "rainy", or "snowy") and suggest an activity.

go

```go
package main

import "fmt"

func main() {
    var weather string
    fmt.Println("What's the weather like today? ('sunny', 'rainy', 'snowy')")
    fmt.Scanln(&weather)
    if weather == "sunny" {
        fmt.Println("Great! Let's go to the park!")
    } else if weather == "rainy" {
        fmt.Println("Don't forget your umbrella!")
    } else if weather == "snowy" {
        fmt.Println("Time to build a snowman!")
    } else {
        fmt.Println("Hmm, I don't recognize that weather.")
    }
}
```

1.

Note to Parents and Teachers:

At this stage, children are learning the basics of control flow in programming. Encouraging them to think about conditions and outcomes helps develop logical thinking and problem-solving skills. Working through examples together can make learning more interactive and enjoyable.

Great job, budding programmer! ☐ You've learned how to make your programs think and make decisions, just like you do every day. In the next chapter, we'll explore loops and learn how to repeat actions efficiently. Keep up the amazing work!

Chapter 7: Loop-de-Loop: Doing Things Over and Over

Let's Go in Circles with Loops

Hello again, coding explorer! Have you ever noticed how some things happen over and over again? Like the wheels on a bike turning as you pedal, or the hands of a clock moving around the face? In programming, we often need to repeat actions multiple times, and we can do this easily using something called **loops**.

What Is a Loop?

A **loop** is a way to tell the computer to do something again and again, until we say stop. It's like telling your friend:

- "Clap your hands 5 times."
- "Jump up and down until I say stop."

In Go, we can use loops to make our code repeat actions, which can save us from writing the same lines over and over.

Why Use Loops?

- **Save Time**: Instead of writing the same code many times, we can write it once and loop it.
- **Automate Tasks**: Loops can handle repetitive tasks without getting tired (computers don't get tired!).
-

Fun Patterns: We can create interesting patterns and effects by repeating actions.

Counting with For Loops

In Go, the most common type of loop is the **for loop**. Let's learn how to use it!

The For Loop Structure

A basic for loop in Go looks like this:

go

```
for i := 1; i <= 5; i++ {

    // Code to repeat

}
```

Let's break it down:

- **for**: This tells Go we're starting a loop.
- **i := 1**: We start with a variable i set to 1. This is our counter.
- **i <= 5**: We loop as long as i is less than or equal to 5.
- **i++**: After each loop, we add 1 to i. This is like saying i = i + 1.
- **{ ... }**: The code inside the curly braces {} is what we repeat.

Let's See It in Action!

Example 1: Saying Hello Five Times

Let's write a program that says "Hello!" five times.

go

```
package main

import "fmt"

func main() {
    for i := 1; i <= 5; i++ {
        fmt.Println("Hello!")
    }
}
```

Run the Code

When you run this code, you'll see:

Hello!

Hello!

Hello!

Hello!

Hello!

The for loop made the computer print "Hello!" five times!

Understanding the Counter Variable i

- The variable i is our **counter**.

- It starts at 1 (i := 1).
- Each time the loop runs, i increases by 1 (i++).
- The loop stops when i becomes greater than 5.

We can even print the value of i to see how it changes.

Example 2: Counting from 1 to 5

go

```
package main
import "fmt"
func main() {
    for i := 1; i <= 5; i++ {
        fmt.Println("Count:", i)
    }
}
```

Output

makefile

Count: 1

Count: 2

Count: 3

Count: 4

Count: 5

Let's Make It More Fun!

Example 3: Multiplication Table

Let's create a simple multiplication table for the number 2.

```go
package main

import "fmt"

func main() {
    fmt.Println(" Multiplication Table for 2")
    for i := 1; i <= 10; i++ {
        result := 2 * i
        fmt.Println("2 x", i, "=", result)
    }
}
```

Output

```css
Multiplication Table for 2
2 x 1 = 2
2 x 2 = 4
2 x 3 = 6
```

2 x 4 = 8

2 x 5 = 10

2 x 6 = 12

2 x 7 = 14

2 x 8 = 16

2 x 9 = 18

2 x 10 = 20

Explaining the Code

- We use `for i := 1; i <= 10; i++` to loop from 1 to 10.
- Inside the loop, we calculate `result := 2 * i`.
- We print out the multiplication in each step.

Nested Loops: Loops Inside Loops

Sometimes, we can put one loop inside another loop. This is called a **nested loop**.

Example 4: Drawing a Square of Stars

Let's draw a square made of stars *.

go

package main

import "fmt"

```
func main() {
    for i := 1; i <= 5; i++ {
        for j := 1; j <= 5; j++ {
            fmt.Print("*")
        }
        fmt.Println()
    }
}
```

Output

```markdown
*****
*****
*****
*****
*****
```

Understanding Nested Loops

- The outer loop (i) runs 5 times.
- For each iteration of the outer loop, the inner loop (j) runs 5 times.
- fmt.Print("*") prints a star without moving to a new line.
-

fmt.Println() moves to the next line after the inner loop finishes.

Infinite Loops: Be Careful!

An **infinite loop** is a loop that never stops. We need to be careful to set conditions that will eventually end the loop.

Example of an Infinite Loop (Don't Run This!)

```go
package main

import "fmt"

func main() {
    i := 1
    for {
        fmt.Println("This will run forever!", i)
        i++
    }
}
```

- This loop has no condition to stop, so it will keep running forever.
- To stop an infinite loop in your program, you might need to close the program or stop it manually.

Practice Time!

Activity 1: Counting Down

Let's write a program that counts down from 5 to 1.

go

```
package main

import "fmt"

func main() {
    for i := 5; i >= 1; i-- {
        fmt.Println("Countdown:", i)
    }
    fmt.Println("Blast off!")
}
```

Output

vbnet

Countdown: 5

Countdown: 4

Countdown: 3

Countdown: 2

Countdown: 1

Blast off!

Activity 2: Even Numbers

Print all even numbers between 1 and 10.

go

```go
package main

import "fmt"

func main() {
    fmt.Println("Even numbers between 1 and 10:")
    for i := 1; i <= 10; i++ {
        if i%2 == 0 {
            fmt.Println(i)
        }
    }
}
```

Output

sql

```
Even numbers between 1 and 10:
2
4
6
8
```

- **Note**: i%2 means the remainder when i is divided by 2. If the remainder is 0, the number is even.

Activity 3: Triangle of Stars

Create a triangle using stars.

go

```
package main

import "fmt"

func main() {
    for i := 1; i <= 5; i++ {
        for j := 1; j <= i; j++ {
            fmt.Print("*")
        }
        fmt.Println()
    }
}
```

Output

markdown

*

**

```
***
****
*****
```

What Did We Learn?

- **For Loops**: How to repeat actions using for loops.
- **Loop Counters**: Using variables like i to keep track of loop iterations.
- **Nested Loops**: Placing one loop inside another to create patterns.
- **Loop Conditions**: Ensuring loops have proper start and end conditions to avoid infinite loops.
- **Modulo Operator %**: Using % to find remainders, helpful in finding even or odd numbers.

Tips for Success:

- **Increment and Decrement**: i++ adds 1 to i each time. i-- subtracts 1.
- **Be Careful with Conditions**: Make sure your loop conditions will eventually stop the loop.
- **Experiment**: Try changing the numbers in your loops to see what happens.

Challenge Time!

1. **FizzBuzz Game**

   ○

   For numbers from 1 to 15:

   - If the number is divisible by 3, print "Fizz".
   - If it's divisible by 5, print "Buzz".
   - If it's divisible by both 3 and 5, print "FizzBuzz".
   - Otherwise, just print the number.

go

```go
package main

import "fmt"

func main() {
    for i := 1; i <= 15; i++ {
        if i%3 == 0 && i%5 == 0 {
            fmt.Println("FizzBuzz")
        } else if i%3 == 0 {
            fmt.Println("Fizz")
        } else if i%5 == 0 {
            fmt.Println("Buzz")
```

```
    } else {
        fmt.Println(i)
    }
  }
}
```

Output:

1

2

Fizz

4

Buzz

Fizz

7

8

Fizz

Buzz

11

Fizz

13

14

FizzBuzz

1.

Creating a Number Pyramid

go

```
package main

import "fmt"

func main() {
   for i := 1; i <= 5; i++ {
      for j := 1; j <= i; j++ {
         fmt.Print(j, " ")
      }
      fmt.Println()
   }
}
```

Output:

1
1 2
1 2 3
1 2 3 4
1 2 3 4 5

1.

2. **Custom Message Repeater**
   o

   Ask the user for a message and how many times to repeat it.

go

```
package main

import "fmt"

func main() {

    var message string

    var times int

    fmt.Println("Enter a message:")

    fmt.Scanln(&message)

    fmt.Println("How many times do you want to repeat it?")

    fmt.Scanln(&times)

    for i := 1; i <= times; i++ {

        fmt.Println(message)

    }

}
```

1. **Note:** As before, fmt.Scanln won't work in the Go Playground. You'll need to run this code on your computer.

Note to Parents and Teachers:

Loops are a fundamental concept in programming. They help children understand how computers can perform repetitive tasks efficiently. Encouraging kids to create patterns or simple games using loops can make learning more engaging.

Great job, coding superstar! ☐ You've learned how to make your programs repeat actions using loops, making them more powerful and efficient. In the next chapter, we'll explore **Fantastic Functions**, where we'll learn how to create our own magic tricks in code. Keep up the excellent work!

Chapter 8: Fantastic Functions

Magic Tricks Called Functions

Hello, magical coder! Have you ever wished you could perform magic tricks? In programming, we have our own kind of magic called **functions**. Functions help us organize our code, perform tasks, and make our programs smarter and more fun.

What Is a Function?

A **function** is like a magic spell or a recipe. It's a set of instructions that tells the computer how to do something. You can think of it as a special box:

- You give it something (inputs).
- It does some magic inside (code).
- It gives you something back (output).

Imagine a machine where you put in flour and eggs, and out comes a cake! □ That's what a function does in code.

Why Use Functions?

- **Reuse Code**: Write code once and use it many times.
- **Organize Your Program**: Keep your code neat and tidy.
- **Make Coding Easier**: Break big problems into smaller, manageable pieces.

Creating Your Own Functions

Let's learn how to create our own functions and see the magic happen!

The Basic Structure of a Function

In Go, we define a function using the `func` keyword, followed by the function's name, any inputs in parentheses, and the code inside curly braces `{}`.

```go
func functionName() {
    // Code to do something
}
```

Let's make a simple function together.

Example 1: A Function That Says Hello

Let's create a function that says "Hello, World!" when we call it.

```go
package main

import "fmt"

func sayHello() {
    fmt.Println("Hello, World!")
}

func main() {
```

```
    sayHello()

}
```

What's Happening Here?

- **func sayHello() { ... }**: We define a function named sayHello. It doesn't take any inputs.
- Inside the function, we have fmt.Println("Hello, World!"), which prints the message.
- In the main function, we call sayHello() to perform the magic.

Run the Code

When you run this code, you'll see:

Hello, World!

Calling the Function Multiple Times

We can use our magic spell as many times as we like!

go

```
func main() {

    sayHello()

    sayHello()

    sayHello()

}
```

Output:

Hello, World!

Hello, World!

Hello, World!

Functions with Inputs (Parameters)

Functions can take inputs, called **parameters**, to make them more flexible.

Example 2: Greeting Someone by Name

Let's make a function that greets someone by their name.

go

```
package main

import "fmt"

func greet(name string) {
    fmt.Println("Hello,", name, "!")
}

func main() {
    greet("Lily")
    greet("Max")
    greet("Olivia")
}
```

What's Happening Here?

-

- **func greet(name string) { ... }**: We define a function greet that takes one input name, which is a string.
- Inside the function, we print a greeting using the name.
- In main, we call greet with different names.

Output:

mathematica

Hello, Lily !

Hello, Max !

Hello, Olivia !

Functions with Outputs (Return Values)

Functions can also give us something back using the return keyword.

Example 3: Adding Two Numbers

Let's create a function that adds two numbers and returns the result.

```go
package main

import "fmt"

func addNumbers(a int, b int) int {
    sum := a + b
    return sum
```

}

```
func main() {
    result := addNumbers(5, 3)
    fmt.Println("The sum is", result)
}
```

What's Happening Here?

- **func addNumbers(a int, b int) int { ... }**: We define a function that takes two integers, a and b, and returns an integer.
- We calculate sum := a + b and then return sum.
- In main, we call addNumbers(5, 3) and store the result in result.
- We print the result.

Output:

python

The sum is 8

Simplifying Parameter Types

If multiple parameters have the same type, we can write it like this:

go

func addNumbers(a, b int) int {

```go
    return a + b
}
```

Functions Are Like Magic Spells

Think of functions as magic spells you can cast in your code. Each spell (function) can do something amazing, and you can use it whenever you need.

Practice Time!

Activity 1: Multiplying Numbers

Create a function that multiplies two numbers.

```go
package main

import "fmt"

func multiplyNumbers(a, b int) int {
    return a * b
}

func main() {
    product := multiplyNumbers(4, 5)
    fmt.Println("The product is", product)
}
```

Output:

csharp

The product is 20

Activity 2: Checking for Even Numbers

Write a function that checks if a number is even.

go

```go
package main

import "fmt"

func isEven(number int) bool {
    if number%2 == 0 {
        return true
    } else {
        return false
    }
}

func main() {
    num := 7
    if isEven(num) {
        fmt.Println(num, "is even.")
    } else {
        fmt.Println(num, "is odd.")
    }
}
```

}

Output:

csharp

7 is odd.

Activity 3: Personalized Greetings

Create a function that greets a person with a custom message.

go

```
package main

import "fmt"

func customGreet(name string, message string) {
    fmt.Println(message, name)
}

func main() {
    customGreet("Ava", "Welcome")
    customGreet("Ethan", "Good morning")
    customGreet("Sophia", "Hi there")
}
```

Output:

Welcome Ava

Good morning Ethan

Hi there Sophia

Challenge Time!

Challenge 1: Calculating the Area of a Rectangle

Write a function that calculates and returns the area of a rectangle.

go

```
package main

import "fmt"

func calculateArea(length, width int) int {
    area := length * width
    return area
}

func main() {
    length := 6
    width := 4
    area := calculateArea(length, width)
    fmt.Println("The area of the rectangle is", area)
}
```

Output:

csharp

The area of the rectangle is 24

Challenge 2: Finding the Biggest Number

Create a function that returns the larger of two numbers.

go

```
package main

import "fmt"

func maxNumber(a, b int) int {
    if a > b {
        return a
    } else {
        return b
    }
}
func main() {
    bigger := maxNumber(9, 12)
    fmt.Println("The bigger number is", bigger)
}
```

Output:

csharp

The bigger number is 12

Challenge 3: Creating a Simple Calculator

Write functions for addition, subtraction, multiplication, and division.

go

```go
package main

import "fmt"

func add(a, b int) int {
    return a + b
}

func subtract(a, b int) int {
    return a - b
}

func multiply(a, b int) int {
    return a * b
}

func divide(a, b int) int {
    return a / b
}

func main() {
    num1 := 20
    num2 := 4
    fmt.Println("Addition:", add(num1, num2))
```

```
fmt.Println("Subtraction:", subtract(num1, num2))

fmt.Println("Multiplication:", multiply(num1, num2))

fmt.Println("Division:", divide(num1, num2))
}
```

Output:

makefile

Addition: 24

Subtraction: 16

Multiplication: 80

Division: 5

What Did We Learn?

- **Functions**: How to define and use functions in Go.
- **Parameters**: Passing inputs to functions to make them flexible.
- **Return Values**: Getting outputs from functions.
- **Reusing Code**: Writing code once and using it many times.
- **Organizing Code**: Keeping our programs neat and easy to understand.

Tips for Success:

- **Choose Clear Names**: Use descriptive names for your functions and variables.
- **One Task per Function**: Each function should do one thing well.
- **Test Your Functions**: Try different inputs to make sure your functions work correctly.

Note to Parents and Teachers:

Functions are essential in programming. They help children understand how to break down problems into smaller, manageable pieces. Encourage kids to think about tasks they can turn into functions and to practice writing their own.

Great job, coding magician! ☐ You've learned how to create your own magic tricks with functions. This powerful tool will help you build bigger and better programs. In the next chapter, we'll explore **Collections of Fun: Arrays and Slices**, where we'll learn how to handle lists of data. Keep up the fantastic work!

Chapter 9: Collections of Fun: Arrays and Slices

Keeping Track of Many Things

Hello again, awesome coder! Have you ever collected things like stickers, toy cars, or shells from the beach? When you have a collection, it's fun to keep them organized so you can find them easily. In programming, we sometimes need to keep track of many pieces of data, like numbers or words. That's where **arrays** and **slices** come into play!

What Are Arrays?

An **array** is like a box with compartments, where each compartment holds one item. Imagine a chocolate box with different chocolates in each slot. In Go, an array is a collection of items of the **same type** (like all numbers or all strings) and has a fixed size.

Let's See an Array

Here's how we create an array in Go:

```go
package main

import "fmt"

func main() {
    var numbers [5]int
    fmt.Println(numbers)
```

}

What's Happening Here?

- **var numbers [5]int**: We declare an array named numbers that can hold 5 integers (int).

- **fmt.Println(numbers)**: We print the array to see what's inside.

Output:

csharp

[0 0 0 0 0]

- The array starts with all zeros because we haven't added any numbers yet.

Adding Items to an Array

Let's fill our array with some numbers!

go

```
package main

import "fmt"

func main() {
    var numbers [5]int
    numbers[0] = 10
    numbers[1] = 20
```

```
numbers[2] = 30

numbers[3] = 40

numbers[4] = 50

fmt.Println(numbers)
}
```

What's Happening Here?

- **numbers[0] = 10**: We assign the value 10 to the first slot in the array. Arrays in Go start counting from **0**.
- We fill the rest of the array with values.
- **fmt.Println(numbers)**: We print the array.

Output:

csharp

[10 20 30 40 50]

Accessing Items in an Array

We can access individual items by their index (position in the array).

go

```
fmt.Println(numbers[2])
```

Output:

30

- numbers[2] gives us the third item (remember, we start counting from 0).

Limitations of Arrays

- **Fixed Size**: Once we create an array of a certain size, we can't change it.
- **Same Type**: All items must be of the same type.

Playing with Lists

To make our collections more flexible, Go provides something called **slices**. Slices are like arrays but better! They can change in size, and we can add or remove items easily.

What Are Slices?

A **slice** is like a dynamic list that can grow or shrink as needed. It's like having a magic bag that can hold any number of items.

Creating a Slice

Method 1: Using [] Without Size

go

package main

import "fmt"

func main() {

    var numbers []int

fmt.Println(numbers)

}

- We declare a slice numbers without specifying a size.

Output:

css

[]

Adding Items to a Slice

We can use the **append** function to add items to a slice.

go

package main

import "fmt"

func main() {

  var numbers []int

  numbers = append(numbers, 10)

  numbers = append(numbers, 20)

  numbers = append(numbers, 30)

  fmt.Println(numbers)

}

Output:

csharp

[10 20 30]

Accessing Items in a Slice

Just like arrays, we can access items by their index.

go

fmt.Println(numbers[1])

Output:

20

Looping Through a Slice

We can use a loop to go through each item in a slice.

go

```
package main

import "fmt"

func main() {
    numbers := []int{10, 20, 30, 40, 50}
    for i := 0; i < len(numbers); i++ {
        fmt.Println("Item", i, "is", numbers[i])
    }
}
```

Output:

```csharp
Item 0 is 10
Item 1 is 20
Item 2 is 30
Item 3 is 40
Item 4 is 50
```

- **len(numbers)** gives us the length (number of items) in the slice.

A Fun Example: Favorite Fruits

Let's create a slice to store your favorite fruits.

```go
package main

import "fmt"

func main() {
    fruits := []string{}
    fruits = append(fruits, "Apple")
    fruits = append(fruits, "Banana")
    fruits = append(fruits, "Cherry")
    fmt.Println("My favorite fruits are:")
    for i := 0; i < len(fruits); i++ {
```

```go
        fmt.Println("-", fruits[i])
    }
}
```

Output:

```diff
My favorite fruits are:
- Apple
- Banana
- Cherry
```

Slices Are Dynamic!

We can add or remove items from slices at any time.

Adding More Fruits

```go
fruits = append(fruits, "Date")
fruits = append(fruits, "Elderberry")
```

Removing Items (Advanced)

Removing items from a slice requires a bit more code.

```go
// Remove the second item (Banana)
fruits = append(fruits[:1], fruits[2:]...)
```

- **Note**: This is a bit advanced. For now, focus on adding items.

Using Range in Loops

We can simplify our loop using range.

```go
for index, fruit := range fruits {
    fmt.Println("Fruit", index, "is", fruit)
}
```

Output:

```vbnet
Fruit 0 is Apple
Fruit 1 is Cherry
Fruit 2 is Date
Fruit 3 is Elderberry
```

Practice Time!

Activity 1: Shopping List

Create a program to manage a shopping list.

```go
package main
```

```go
import "fmt"

func main() {
    shoppingList := []string{}
    shoppingList = append(shoppingList, "Milk")
    shoppingList = append(shoppingList, "Bread")
    shoppingList = append(shoppingList, "Eggs")
    fmt.Println("Shopping List:")
    for _, item := range shoppingList {
        fmt.Println("-", item)
    }
}
```

Output:

diff

Shopping List:

- Milk

- Bread

- Eggs

Activity 2: Number Collection

Store numbers from 1 to 10 in a slice and calculate their sum.

go

```go
package main

import "fmt"

func main() {
    numbers := []int{}
    sum := 0
    for i := 1; i <= 10; i++ {
        numbers = append(numbers, i)
        sum += i
    }
    fmt.Println("Numbers:", numbers)
    fmt.Println("Sum:", sum)
}
```

Output:

makefile

Numbers: [1 2 3 4 5 6 7 8 9 10]

Sum: 55

Activity 3: Class Attendance

Keep track of students present in a class.

go

package main

```go
import "fmt"

func main() {
    students := []string{"Alice", "Bob", "Charlie"}
    fmt.Println("Students present today:")
    for _, student := range students {
        fmt.Println("-", student)
    }
    // Adding a new student
    students = append(students, "Diana")
    fmt.Println("\nUpdated list:")
    for _, student := range students {
        fmt.Println("-", student)
    }
}
```

Output:

```diff
Students present today:
- Alice
- Bob
- Charlie
```

Updated list:

- Alice

- Bob

- Charlie

- Diana

Challenge Time!

Challenge 1: High Scores

Create a program that keeps track of high scores in a game.

go

```
package main
import "fmt"
func main() {
    highScores := []int{}
    // Adding scores
    highScores = append(highScores, 100)
    highScores = append(highScores, 200)
    highScores = append(highScores, 150)
    fmt.Println("High Scores:")
    for _, score := range highScores {
        fmt.Println(score)
```

        }
    }

Output:

yaml

High Scores:

100

200

150

Challenge 2: Favorite Colors

Ask the user for their favorite colors and store them in a slice.

go

```
package main

import "fmt"

func main() {
    var colors []string
    var color string
    fmt.Println("Enter your favorite colors (type 'done' to finish):")
    for {
        fmt.Scanln(&color)
        if color == "done" {
```

```go
            break
        }
        colors = append(colors, color)
    }
    fmt.Println("Your favorite colors are:")
    for _, c := range colors {
        fmt.Println("-", c)
    }
}
```

- **Note**: This code requires input from the user and should be run on your computer.

Challenge 3: Animal List Sorting (Advanced)

Create a program that sorts a list of animals.

go

```go
package main

import (
    "fmt"
    "sort"
)

func main() {
```

```go
animals := []string{"Zebra", "Elephant", "Lion", "Giraffe"}
fmt.Println("Unsorted Animals:")
for _, animal := range animals {
    fmt.Println("-", animal)
}
// Sorting the slice
sort.Strings(animals)
fmt.Println("\nSorted Animals:")
for _, animal := range animals {
    fmt.Println("-", animal)
}
}
```

Output:

diff

Unsorted Animals:

- Zebra

- Elephant

- Lion

- Giraffe

Sorted Animals:

- Elephant

- Giraffe

- Lion

- Zebra

-

Note: We use the sort package to sort the slice.

What Did We Learn?

- Arrays: Fixed-size collections of items of the same type.
- Slices: Dynamic lists that can grow or shrink.
- Creating and Using Slices: How to declare, append items, and access elements.
- Looping Through Collections: Using loops to go through arrays and slices.
- Indexing: Accessing items by their position.
- Range Loop: A simple way to loop through slices.

Tips for Success:

- Remember Indexing Starts at 0: The first item is at index 0.
-

Use Slices for Flexibility: Prefer slices over arrays when you need a dynamic collection.

-

Practice Makes Perfect: Try creating your own slices with different data types.

Note to Parents and Teachers:

Understanding collections like arrays and slices is fundamental in programming. They allow children to manage groups of data efficiently. Encouraging kids to think of real-world collections (like toy boxes or sticker albums) can help make these concepts more relatable.

Great job, coding collector! You've learned how to keep track of many things using arrays and slices. Now you can organize data in your programs just like organizing your favorite collections. In the next chapter, we'll explore **Strings: Words and Sentences**, where we'll have fun playing with text and learning how to manipulate words in code. Keep up the excellent work!

Chapter 10: Strings: Words and Sentences

Talking in Code

Hello, young linguist! Did you know that computers can understand words and sentences too? In programming, we use something called **strings** to work with text. A **string** is a sequence of characters—like letters, numbers, and symbols—all bundled together.

Imagine strings as beads on a necklace. Each bead is a character, and the whole necklace is the string! □

What Is a String?

In Go, a string is a way to store and manipulate text. We put the text inside double quotes " ".

Example:

```go
message := "Hello, world!"
```

Here, message is a variable that holds the string "Hello, world!".

Let's Try It!

Let's write a program that uses strings.

```go
package main
```

```
import "fmt"

func main() {
    greeting := "Hello"
    name := "Sam"
    fmt.Println(greeting + ", " + name + "!")
}
```

What's Happening Here?

- We have two string variables:
  - greeting holds "Hello".
  - name holds "Sam".
- We use the + operator to **concatenate** (join) the strings together.
- The fmt.Println prints the combined string.

Output:

Hello, Sam!

Fun with Words and Letters

Now, let's have some fun playing with strings!

Concatenation: Joining Strings Together

As we saw, we can join strings using the + operator.

Example:

```go
firstName := "Alex"
lastName := "Johnson"
fullName := firstName + " " + lastName
fmt.Println("Full Name:", fullName)
```

Output:

```mathematica
Full Name: Alex Johnson
```

String Length: How Many Characters?

We can find out how long a string is using the len() function.

Example:

```go
word := "Gopher"
length := len(word)
fmt.Println("The word", word, "has", length, "letters.")
```

Output:

```arduino
The word Gopher has 6 letters.
```

Accessing Individual Characters

Strings are like slices of characters. We can access individual characters using their index.

Example:

go

word := "Go"

firstLetter := word[0]

secondLetter := word[1]

fmt.Println("First letter:", string(firstLetter))

fmt.Println("Second letter:", string(secondLetter))

Output:

sql

First letter: G

Second letter: o

- **Note:** We use string() to convert the byte to a string character.

Looping Through a String

We can loop through each character in a string.

Example:

go

text := "Hello"

```
for i := 0; i < len(text); i++ {
    fmt.Println("Character at position", i, "is", string(text[i]))
}
```

Output:

arduino

Character at position 0 is H

Character at position 1 is e

Character at position 2 is l

Character at position 3 is l

Character at position 4 is o

String Formatting

We can use fmt.Printf to format strings in different ways.

Example:

go

name := "Taylor"

age := 10

fmt.Printf("My name is %s and I am %d years old.\n", name, age)

- %s is a placeholder for a string.
- %d is a placeholder for an integer.
-

\n is a newline character, which moves the cursor to the next line.

Output:

csharp

My name is Taylor and I am 10 years old.

Fun String Functions

Go has many functions to manipulate strings.

Converting to Uppercase or Lowercase

We can change all letters to uppercase or lowercase.

```go
import (
    "fmt"
    "strings"
)
func main() {
    text := "Hello, World!"
    upperText := strings.ToUpper(text)
    lowerText := strings.ToLower(text)
    fmt.Println("Original:", text)
    fmt.Println("Uppercase:", upperText)
    fmt.Println("Lowercase:", lowerText)
```

}

Output:

makefile

Original: Hello, World!

Uppercase: HELLO, WORLD!

Lowercase: hello, world!

Checking If a String Contains Another String

We can check if one string is part of another.

```go
import (
    "fmt"
    "strings"
)
func main() {
    sentence := "The quick brown fox jumps over the lazy dog"
    word := "fox"
    if strings.Contains(sentence, word) {
        fmt.Println("The sentence contains the word:", word)
    } else {
        fmt.Println("The word is not in the sentence.")
```

        }
}

Output:

arduino

The sentence contains the word: fox

Splitting Strings

We can split a string into a slice of strings.

go

import (

   "fmt"

   "strings"

)

func main() {

   sentence := "Go is fun"

   words := strings.Split(sentence, " ")

   fmt.Println("Words:", words)

}

Output:

kotlin

Words: [Go is fun]

Joining Strings

We can join a slice of strings into one string.

```go
import (
    "fmt"
    "strings"
)

func main() {
    words := []string{"Learning", "to", "code", "is", "awesome"}
    sentence := strings.Join(words, " ")
    fmt.Println("Sentence:", sentence)
}
```

Output:

```vbnet
Sentence: Learning to code is awesome
```

Replacing Parts of a String

We can replace parts of a string with something else.

```go
import (
    "fmt"
```

```go
    "strings"
)

func main() {
    original := "I like cats"
    modified := strings.ReplaceAll(original, "cats", "dogs")
    fmt.Println("Original:", original)
    fmt.Println("Modified:", modified)
}
```

Output:

```vbnet
Original: I like cats
Modified: I like dogs
```

Practice Time!

Activity 1: Palindrome Checker

A palindrome is a word that reads the same backward and forward.

```go
import (
    "fmt"
    "strings"
)
```

```go
func main() {
    word := "racecar"
    reversedWord := reverseString(word)
    if word == reversedWord {
        fmt.Println(word, "is a palindrome!")
    } else {
        fmt.Println(word, "is not a palindrome.")
    }
}

func reverseString(s string) string {
    runes := []rune(s)
    for i, j := 0, len(runes)-1; i < j; i, j = i+1, j-1 {
        runes[i], runes[j] = runes[j], runes[i]
    }
    return string(runes)
}
```

Output:

csharp

racecar is a palindrome!

Activity 2: Count Vowels

Let's count how many vowels are in a sentence.

```go
import (
    "fmt"
    "strings"
)
func main() {
    text = "Hello, how are you?"
    count := 0
    vowels := "aeiouAEIOU"
    for _, char := range text {
        if strings.ContainsRune(vowels, char) {
            count++
        }
    }
    fmt.Println("Number of vowels: ', count)
}
```

Output:

javascript

Number of vowels: 7

Activity 3: Silly Sentence Maker

Let's create a silly sentence by combining words.

go

```
import "fmt"

func main() {
    adjective := "fuzzy"
    animal := "unicorn"
    place := "moon"
    sentence := "The " + adjective + " " + animal + " danced on the " + place + "."
    fmt.Println(sentence)
}
```

Output:

csharp

The fuzzy unicorn danced on the moon.

Challenge Time!

Challenge 1: Word Guessing Game

Create a simple word guessing game.

go

import (

```go
    "fmt"
    "strings"
)

func main() {
    secretWord := "gopher"
    var guess string
    fmt.Println("Guess the secret word:")
    fmt.Scanln(&guess)
    if strings.ToLower(guess) == secretWord {
        fmt.Println("You guessed it!")
    } else {
        fmt.Println("Try again!")
    }
}
```

- **Note:** This code requires user input and should be run on your computer.

Challenge 2: Pig Latin Translator

Translate words into Pig Latin (just for fun!).

```go
import "fmt"
```

```go
func main() {
    word := "gopher"
    pigLatin := word[1:] + string(word[0]) + "ay"
    fmt.Println("Original word:", word)
    fmt.Println("Pig Latin:", pigLatin)
}
```

Output:

yaml

Original word: gopher

Pig Latin: ophergay

Challenge 3: Word Reverser

Reverse the words in a sentence.

```go
import (
    "fmt"
    "strings"
)
func main() {
    sentence := "Go is fun"
    words := strings.Split(sentence, " ")
```

```
    reversedWords := reverseWords(words)

    reversedSentence := strings.Join(reversedWords, " ")

    fmt.Println("Original:", sentence)

    fmt.Println("Reversed:", reversedSentence)

}

func reverseWords(words []string) []string {

    for i, j := 0, len(words)-1; i < j; i, j = i+1, j-1 {

        words[i], words[j] = words[j], words[i]

    }

    return words

}
```

Output:

kotlin

Original: Go is fun

Reversed: fun is Go

What Did We Learn?

- **Strings**: How to use and manipulate text in Go.
- **Concatenation**: Joining strings together using +.
- **String Length**: Using len() to find out how many characters are in a string.

- **Accessing Characters**: Getting individual characters using indexing.
- **String Functions**: Using built-in functions like ToUpper, ToLower, Contains, Split, Join, and ReplaceAll.
- **Formatting Strings**: Using fmt.Printf with placeholders.

Tips for Success:

- **Always Use Double Quotes**: In Go, strings are enclosed in double quotes " ".
- **Escape Characters**: Use \n for a new line, \t for a tab.
- **Practice**: Try creating your own sentences and play with different string functions.

Note to Parents and Teachers:

Understanding strings is essential for programming, as text manipulation is a common task. Encouraging children to experiment with words and sentences can make learning strings enjoyable. Activities like creating silly sentences or simple games can enhance engagement.

Great job, word wizard! □♂□ You've learned how to talk in code using strings and have fun with words and letters. Now you can make your programs more interactive and creative with text. In the next chapter, we'll work on exciting Go coding projects where you'll put everything you've learned into action. Keep up the amazing work!

Chapter 11: Go Coding Projects

Making a Simple Game

Introduction

Hello, superstar coder! ☐ Are you ready to put everything you've learned into action? In this chapter, we'll work on some exciting projects that will show you how to create simple games, fun quizzes, and even draw shapes with code! Let's start by making a simple game.

Our Simple Guessing Game

We're going to create a **Number Guessing Game** where the computer thinks of a secret number, and you try to guess it!

Setting Up the Game

Step 1: Plan the Game

- The computer picks a secret number between 1 and 10.
- You try to guess the number.
- The computer tells you if your guess is too high, too low, or correct.
- You can keep guessing until you get it right.

Step 2: Writing the Code

Let's start coding! Open your Go Playground or coding editor.

go

```go
package main

import (
    "fmt"
    "math/rand"
    "time"
)

func main() {
    rand.Seed(time.Now().UnixNano()) // Seed the random number generator
    secretNumber := rand.Intn(10) + 1 // Generate a number between 1 and 10
    var guess int
    fmt.Println("I'm thinking of a number between 1 and 10.")
    fmt.Println("Can you guess what it is?")
    for {
        fmt.Print("Enter your guess: ")
        fmt.Scanln(&guess)
        if guess == secretNumber {
            fmt.Println("You got it! ")
```

```go
            break
        } else if guess < secretNumber {
            fmt.Println("Too low! Try again.")
        } else {
            fmt.Println("Too high! Try again.")
        }
    }
}
```

Understanding the Code

Importing Packages
```go
import (
    "fmt"
    "math/rand"
    "time"
)
```

-
  - **"fmt"**: Allows us to print messages and get user input.
  - **"math/rand"**: Lets us generate random numbers.
  -

"**time**": Used to seed the random number generator.

Seeding the Random Number Generator

go

rand.Seed(time.Now().UnixNano())

-
  - This ensures we get a different random number each time we play.

Generating the Secret Number

go

secretNumber := rand.Intn(10) + 1

-
  - rand.Intn(10) generates a random number between 0 and 9.
  - Adding + 1 makes it between 1 and 10.

Getting User Input

go

fmt.Scanln(&guess)

-
  - Waits for the player to type a number and press Enter.

The Loop

```go
for {
    // Game code
}
```

-
  - The loop continues until the player guesses the correct number.

Checking the Guess

```go
if guess == secretNumber {
    fmt.Println("You got it! ")
    break
} else if guess < secretNumber {
    fmt.Println("Too low! Try again.")
} else {
    fmt.Println("Too high! Try again.")
}
```

-
  - If the guess is correct, we congratulate the player and break out of the loop.
  -

If the guess is too low or too high, we give a hint.

Running the Game

- **Note**: Since the Go Playground doesn't support rand.Seed(time.Now().UnixNano()) or user input (fmt.Scanln), you will need to run this code on your computer.

- **Ask an adult to help you set up Go on your computer if you haven't already.**

Making It More Fun

Limit the Number of Guesses
You can add a variable to count the number of attempts and limit it.

```go
attempts := 0

maxAttempts := 5

for attempts < maxAttempts {

    // Game code

    attempts++

}
```

-

Adding Encouraging Messages
Add messages when the player runs out of guesses.

```go
```

```
if attempts == maxAttempts {

    fmt.Println("Sorry, you've used all your guesses. The number was", secretNumber)

    break

}
```

-

Project Summary

Congratulations! You've created your very own guessing game. This project helps you practice:

- Generating random numbers.
- Using loops and conditions.
- Getting user input.
- Making interactive programs.

Creating a Fun Quiz

Introduction

Now let's create a fun quiz to test your friends and family! We'll ask questions and check if the answers are correct.

Planning the Quiz

- Prepare a few questions and their answers.
- Ask the player each question.
- Check if the player's answer matches the correct answer.
- Keep track of the score.
- Give the final score at the end.

Writing the Code

Step 1: Creating Questions and Answers

We'll use slices to store our questions and answers.

go

```
package main

import "fmt"

func main() {
    questions := []string{
        "What is the capital of France?",
        "What is 5 + 7?",
        "What color do you get when you mix red and white?",
    }
    answers := []string{
        "Paris",
```

```
    "12",
    "Pink",
}
score := 0
var userAnswer string
fmt.Println("Welcome to the Fun Quiz!")
fmt.Println("-----------------------")
for i := 0; i < len(questions); i++ {
    fmt.Println(questions[i])
    fmt.Scanln(&userAnswer)
    if userAnswer == answers[i] {
        fmt.Println("Correct! ")
        score++
    } else {
        fmt.Println("Oops! The correct answer is:", answers[i])
    }
    fmt.Println()
}
fmt.Println("Quiz Over! Your score is:", score, "out of", len(questions))
}
```

Understanding the Code

Questions and Answers Slices

```go
questions := []string{ /* ... */ }

answers := []string{ /* ... */ }
```

- We store our questions and answers in slices so we can loop through them.

Looping Through Questions

```go
for i := 0; i < len(questions); i++ {
    // Ask each question
}
```

Getting User Input

```go
fmt.Scanln(&userAnswer)
```

Checking the Answer

```go
if userAnswer == answers[i] {
    // Correct!
```

```go
} else {
    // Incorrect
}
```

-
- **Keeping Score**
  - We increase score by 1 for each correct answer.

Displaying the Final Score
go

```go
fmt.Println("Quiz Over! Your score is:", score, "out of", len(questions))
```

-

Enhancing the Quiz

Accepting Answers in Any Case
The player might type "paris" instead of "Paris". We can make our check case-insensitive.
go

```go
import (
    "fmt"
    "strings"
)
// ...
if strings.EqualFold(userAnswer, answers[i]) {
```

// Correct!

}

-

Adding More Questions

Just add more questions and answers to the slices.

go

```
questions := []string{
    // Existing questions...
    "What is the largest planet in our solar system?",
}

answers := []string{
    // Existing answers...
    "Jupiter",
}
```

-

Providing Multiple Choices

You can format your questions to include options.

go

```
questions := []string{
    "What is the capital of France?\n(a) Berlin\n(b) Paris\n(c) London",
    // ...
}
```

```go
answers := []string{
    "b",
    // ...
}
```

-

Checking for Correct Options

```go
if strings.ToLower(userAnswer) == answers[i] {
    // Correct!
}
```

-

Project Summary

Fantastic! You've created a fun quiz game. This project helps you practice:

- Using slices to store data.
- Looping through collections.
- Getting and checking user input.
- Keeping track of scores.

Drawing Shapes with Code

Introduction

Did you know you can draw shapes using code? Let's explore how to create simple shapes and patterns in the console.

Drawing Shapes with Asterisks (*)

We'll use loops to print out patterns that form shapes.

Project: Drawing a Rectangle

Step 1: Understanding the Plan

- We'll ask the user for the width and height of the rectangle.
- Use nested loops to print the rectangle using *.

Step 2: Writing the Code

```go
package main

import "fmt"

func main() {
    var width, height int
    fmt.Print("Enter the width of the rectangle: ")
    fmt.Scanln(&width)
    fmt.Print("Enter the height of the rectangle: ")
```

```go
    fmt.Scanln(&height)

    fmt.Println("Here is your rectangle:")

    for i := 0; i < height; i++ {

        for j := 0; j < width; j++ {

            fmt.Print("*")

        }

        fmt.Println()

    }

}
```

Understanding the Code

Getting User Input
go

fmt.Scanln(&width)

fmt.Scanln(&height)

•

Nested Loops
go

for i := 0; i < height; i++ {

    for j := 0; j < width; j++ {

        fmt.Print("*")

    }

    fmt.Println()

}

-
  - The outer loop runs height times.
  - The inner loop runs width times.
  - fmt.Print("*") prints * without a new line.
  - fmt.Println() moves to the next line after each row.

Running the Program

- Input the width and height when prompted.
- See the rectangle appear in the console.

Project: Drawing a Triangle

Let's draw a right-angled triangle.

go

package main

import "fmt"

func main() {

    var size int

    fmt.Print("Enter the size of the triangle: ")

    fmt.Scanln(&size)

```
fmt.Println("Here is your triangle:")
for i := 1; i <= size; i++ {
    for j := 1; j <= i; j++ {
        fmt.Print("*")
    }
    fmt.Println()
}
}
```

Understanding the Code

- **Looping to Form a Triangle**
    - The outer loop runs from 1 to size.
    - The inner loop runs from 1 to i, so each row has one more * than the last.

Output Example

If the size is 5, the triangle will look like:

markdown

*

**

***

****

*****

Project: Drawing a Pyramid (Advanced)

Let's draw a centered pyramid.

go

```go
package main

import "fmt"

func main() {
    var rows int
    fmt.Print("Enter the number of rows for the pyramid: ")
    fmt.Scanln(&rows)
    fmt.Println("Here is your pyramid:")
    for i := 1; i <= rows; i++ {
        // Print spaces
        for j := i; j < rows; j++ {
            fmt.Print(" ")
        }
        // Print stars
        for k := 1; k <= (2*i - 1); k++ {
            fmt.Print("*")
        }
```

        fmt.Println()
    }

}

Understanding the Code

- ### Calculating Spaces and Stars
    o For each row, we print spaces to center the pyramid.
    o The number of stars increases by 2 each row (1, 3, 5, ...).

Output Example

If the number of rows is 5, the pyramid will look like:

markdown

```
    *
   ***
  *****
 *******
*********
```

Project Summary

Awesome! You've learned how to draw shapes using code. This project helps you practice:

-

Using loops to create patterns.

- Understanding how nested loops work.

- Working with user input to customize the output.

Wrapping Up

You've completed the Go Coding Projects chapter! Give yourself a big pat on the back.

What We've Achieved

- **Made a Simple Game**: Created a number guessing game to challenge players.
- **Created a Fun Quiz**: Built a quiz to test knowledge and keep scores.
- **Drawn Shapes with Code**: Used loops to draw rectangles, triangles, and pyramids.

Next Steps

- **Experiment**: Try modifying the projects. Can you add new features?
- **Share**: Show your programs to friends and family. Maybe they can play your games!
-

Keep Coding: The more you practice, the better you'll become.

Tip: Remember, coding is like magic—you can create anything you imagine! Keep exploring, keep experimenting, and most importantly, have fun!

Answer

Chapter 11: Go Coding Projects

Making a Simple Game

Introduction

Hello, superstar coder! □ Are you ready to put everything you've learned into action? In this chapter, we'll work on some exciting projects that will show you how to create simple games, fun quizzes, and even draw shapes with code! Let's start by making a simple game.

Our Simple Guessing Game

We're going to create a **Number Guessing Game** where the computer thinks of a secret number, and you try to guess it!

Setting Up the Game

Step 1: Plan the Game

- The computer picks a secret number between 1 and 10.
- You try to guess the number.
- The computer tells you if your guess is too high, too low, or correct.
- You can keep guessing until you get it right.

Step 2: Writing the Code

Let's start coding! Open your Go Playground or coding editor.

```go
package main

import (
    "fmt"
    "math/rand"
    "time"
)

func main() {
    rand.Seed(time.Now().UnixNano()) // Seed the random number generator
    secretNumber := rand.Intn(10) + 1 // Generate a number between 1 and 10
    var guess int
    fmt.Println("I'm thinking of a number between 1 and 10.")
    fmt.Println("Can you guess what it is?")
    for {
        fmt.Print("Enter your guess: ")
        fmt.Scanln(&guess)
        if guess == secretNumber {
            fmt.Println("You got it! ")
```

```go
        break
    } else if guess < secretNumber {
        fmt.Println("Too low! Try again.")
    } else {
        fmt.Println("Too high! Try again.")
    }
  }
}
```

Understanding the Code

Importing Packages

```go
import (
    "fmt"
    "math/rand"
    "time"
)
```

- - **"fmt"**: Allows us to print messages and get user input.
  - **"math/rand"**: Lets us generate random numbers.

"time": Used to seed the random number generator.

Seeding the Random Number Generator

go

rand.Seed(time.Now().UnixNano())

-
  - This ensures we get a different random number each time we play.

Generating the Secret Number

go

secretNumber := rand.Intn(10) + 1

-
  - rand.Intn(10) generates a random number between 0 and 9.
  - Adding + 1 makes it between 1 and 10.

Getting User Input

go

fmt.Scanln(&guess)

-
  - Waits for the player to type a number and press Enter.

The Loop

```go
for {
    // Game code
}
```

-
  - The loop continues until the player guesses the correct number.

Checking the Guess

```go
if guess == secretNumber {
    fmt.Println("You got it! ")
    break
} else if guess < secretNumber {
    fmt.Println("Too low! Try again.")
} else {
    fmt.Println("Too high! Try again ")
}
```

-
  - If the guess is correct, we congratulate the player and break out of the loop.

If the guess is too low or too high, we give a hint.

Running the Game

- **Note**: Since the Go Playground doesn't support rand.Seed(time.Now().UnixNano()) or user input (fmt.Scanln), you will need to run this code on your computer.

- Ask an adult to help you set up Go on your computer if you haven't already.

Making It More Fun

Limit the Number of Guesses
You can add a variable to count the number of attempts and limit it.

```go
attempts := 0

maxAttempts := 5

for attempts < maxAttempts {

    // Game code

    attempts++

}
```

-

Adding Encouraging Messages
Add messages when the player runs out of guesses.
```go
```

```
if attempts == maxAttempts {

    fmt.Println("Sorry, you've used all your guesses. The number was", secretNumber)

    break

}
```

-

Project Summary

Congratulations! You've created your very own guessing game. This project helps you practice:

- Generating random numbers.
- Using loops and conditions.
- Getting user input.
-
    Making interactive programs.

Creating a Fun Quiz

Introduction

Now let's create a fun quiz to test your friends and family! We'll ask questions and check if the answers are correct.

Planning the Quiz

- Prepare a few questions and their answers.
- Ask the player each question.
- Check if the player's answer matches the correct answer.
- Keep track of the score.
- Give the final score at the end.

Writing the Code

Step 1: Creating Questions and Answers

We'll use slices to store our questions and answers.

go

```
package main

import "fmt"

func main() {
    questions := []string{
        "What is the capital of France?",
        "What is 5 + 7?",
        "What color do you get when you mix red and white?",
    }
    answers := []string{
        "Paris",
```

```
        "12",
        "Pink",
    }
    score := 0
    var userAnswer string
    fmt.Println("Welcome to the Fun Quiz!")
    fmt.Println("------------------------")
    for i := 0; i < len(questions); i++ {
        fmt.Println(questions[i])
        fmt.Scanln(&userAnswer)
        if userAnswer == answers[i] {
            fmt.Println("Correct! ")
            score++
        } else {
            fmt.Println("Oops! The correct answer is:", answers[i])
        }
        fmt.Println()
    }
    fmt.Println("Quiz Over! Your score is:", score, "out of", len(questions))
}
```

Understanding the Code

Questions and Answers Slices
```go
questions := []string{ /* ... */ }

answers := []string{ /* ... */ }
```

-
  - We store our questions and answers in slices so we can loop through them.

Looping Through Questions
```go
for i := 0; i < len(questions); i++ {
    // Ask each question
}
```

-

Getting User Input
```go
fmt.Scanln(&userAnswer)
```

-

Checking the Answer
```go
if userAnswer == answers[i] {
    // Correct!
```

```go
} else {
    // Incorrect
}
```

-
-
Keeping Score

We increase score by 1 for each correct answer.

Displaying the Final Score
```go
fmt.Println("Quiz Over! Your score is:", score, "out of", len(questions))
```

-

Enhancing the Quiz

Accepting Answers in Any Case
The player might type "paris" instead of "Paris". We can make our check case-insensitive.
```go
import (
    "fmt"
    "strings"
)
// ...
if strings.EqualFold(userAnswer, answers[i]) {
```

// Correct!

}

-

Adding More Questions
Just add more questions and answers to the slices.

go

questions := []string{

    // Existing questions...

    "What is the largest planet in our solar system?",

}

answers := []string{

    // Existing answers...

    "Jupiter",

}

-

Providing Multiple Choices
You can format your questions to include options.

go

questions := []string{

    "What is the capital of France?\n(a) Berlin\n(b) Paris\n(c) London",

    // ...

}

```go
answers := []string{
    "b",
    // ...
}
```

-

Checking for Correct Options

```go
if strings.ToLower(userAnswer) == answers[i] {
    // Correct!
}
```

-

Project Summary

Fantastic! You've created a fun quiz game. This project helps you practice:

- Using slices to store data.
- Looping through collections.
- Getting and checking user input.
- Keeping track of scores.

Drawing Shapes with Code

Introduction

Did you know you can draw shapes using code? Let's explore how to create simple shapes and patterns in the console.

Drawing Shapes with Asterisks (*)

We'll use loops to print out patterns that form shapes.

Project: Drawing a Rectangle

Step 1: Understanding the Plan

- We'll ask the user for the width and height of the rectangle.
- Use nested loops to print the rectangle using *.

Step 2: Writing the Code

```go
package main

import "fmt"

func main() {
    var width, height int
    fmt.Print("Enter the width of the rectangle: ")
    fmt.Scanln(&width)
    fmt.Print("Enter the height of the rectangle: ")
```

```
fmt.Scanln(&height)

fmt.Println("Here is your rectangle:")

for i := 0; i < height; i++ {

    for j := 0; j < width; j++ {

        fmt.Print("*")

    }

    fmt.Println()

}
}
```

Understanding the Code

Getting User Input
go

fmt.Scanln(&width)

fmt.Scanln(&height)

-

Nested Loops
go

```
for i := 0; i < height; i++ {

    for j := 0; j < width; j++ {

        fmt.Print("*")

    }
```

fmt.Println()

}

-
  - The outer loop runs height times.
  - The inner loop runs width times.
  - fmt.Print("*") prints * without a new line.
  - fmt.Println() moves to the next line after each row.

Running the Program

- Input the width and height when prompted.
- See the rectangle appear in the console.

Project: Drawing a Triangle

Let's draw a right-angled triangle.

go

package main

import "fmt"

func main() {

  var size int

  fmt.Print("Enter the size of the triangle: ")

  fmt.Scanln(&size)

```
fmt.Println("Here is your triangle:")
for i := 1; i <= size; i++ {
    for j := 1; j <= i; j++ {
        fmt.Print("*")
    }
    fmt.Println()
}
}
```

Understanding the Code

- **Looping to Form a Triangle**
  - The outer loop runs from 1 to size.
  - The inner loop runs from 1 to i, so each row has one more * than the last.

Output Example

If the size is 5, the triangle will look like:

markdown

```
*
**
***
****
```

*****

Project: Drawing a Pyramid (Advanced)

Let's draw a centered pyramid.

go

```
package main

import "fmt"

func main() {
    var rows int
    fmt.Print("Enter the number of rows for the pyramid: ")
    fmt.Scanln(&rows)
    fmt.Println("Here is your pyramid:")
    for i := 1; i <= rows; i++ {
        // Print spaces
        for j := i; j < rows; j++ {
            fmt.Print(" ")
        }
        // Print stars
        for k := 1; k <= (2*i - 1); k++ {
            fmt.Print("*")
        }
```

```
    fmt.Println()
  }
}
```

Understanding the Code

- **Calculating Spaces and Stars**
    - For each row, we print spaces to center the pyramid.
    - The number of stars increases by 2 each row (1, 3, 5, ...).

Output Example

If the number of rows is 5, the pyramid will look like:

markdown

```
    *
   ***
  *****
 *******
*********
```

Project Summary

Awesome! You've learned how to draw shapes using code. This project helps you practice:

-

- Using loops to create patterns.
- Understanding how nested loops work.
- Working with user input to customize the output.

Wrapping Up

You've completed the Go Coding Projects chapter! Give yourself a big pat on the back.

What We've Achieved

- **Made a Simple Game**: Created a number guessing game to challenge players.
- **Created a Fun Quiz**: Built a quiz to test knowledge and keep scores.
- **Drawn Shapes with Code**: Used loops to draw rectangles, triangles, and pyramids.

Next Steps

- **Experiment**: Try modifying the projects. Can you add new features?
- **Share**: Show your programs to friends and family. Maybe they can play your games!
-

Keep Coding: The more you practice, the better you'll become.

Tip: Remember, coding is like magic—you can create anything you imagine! Keep exploring, keep experimenting, and most importantly, have fun!

Chapter 12: Your Next Steps in Coding

Exploring More with Go

Hello, future coding superstar! □ You've done an amazing job learning the basics of Go with Go the Gopher. You've written programs, created games, solved puzzles, and even drawn shapes with code. Now, let's talk about how you can continue your coding adventure and explore even more with Go!

Build Bigger and Better Projects

Now that you're comfortable with the basics, why not challenge yourself with bigger projects?

-
  Create a Storybook: Write a program that tells a story and lets the reader make choices that change the ending.
-
  Develop a Mini Calculator: Build a calculator that can add, subtract, multiply, and divide numbers.
-
  Design a Quiz Game: Make a quiz that asks questions and keeps track of the score, just like we did in the projects chapter.

Learn About Go Packages

Go has many packages that can help you do more exciting things.

-

Explore the math **Package**: Learn how to use advanced math functions to calculate square roots, exponents, and more.

-
Use the time **Package**: Create programs that tell the current time or make the program wait before doing something.

-

Discover the net/http **Package**: Start building simple web servers (this might need some adult help).

Dive into Graphics and Games

While Go is great for writing code that runs in the console (the black or white window where you see text), you can also create programs with graphics!

-
Learn Go with Graphics: Use packages like ebiten or fyne to create simple games or applications with pictures and buttons.
-

Make a Drawing App: Build a program where you can draw shapes and lines on the screen.

Collaborate with Others

Coding can be even more fun when you share it with friends.

-
Join a Coding Club: See if your school or community has a coding club where you can learn with others.
-

Share Your Projects: Show your programs to friends and family. Maybe you can teach them how to code too!

Keep Practicing

The best way to get better at coding is to keep practicing.

- **Set Aside Time**: Try to code a little bit each day or each week.
- **Keep a Coding Journal**: Write down ideas for programs you want to make or things you want to learn.
- **Challenge Yourself**: Try solving coding puzzles or finding online challenges suitable for your age.

Other Fun Coding Languages to Try

While Go is an awesome language, there are many other programming languages out there that are fun to learn. Each language has its own special features and is used for different things. Let's take a look at some you might enjoy.

Scratch

- **What Is Scratch?**
    - Scratch is a visual programming language created by MIT. It uses colorful blocks that you snap together to create animations, games, and stories.
- **Why Try Scratch?**
    - It's perfect for beginners and helps you understand programming concepts without writing code.
- **How to Get Started:**
    -

Visit the Scratch website and start creating right away.

Python

- **What Is Python?**
  - Python is a popular language known for being easy to read and write.
- **Why Try Python?**
  - It's used in many areas, like web development, science, and even making games.
- **How to Get Started:**
  - There are many kid-friendly books and tutorials on Python. Check out Python for Kids.

JavaScript

- **What Is JavaScript?**
  - JavaScript is the language of the web. It makes websites interactive.
- **Why Try JavaScript?**
  - You can create fun web pages, games, and apps that run in a browser.
- **How to Get Started:**
  - Try tutorials on Code.org or Khan Academy.

Blockly

- ### What Is Blockly?
  - Blockly is similar to Scratch but allows you to see the actual code behind the blocks.
- ### Why Try Blockly?
  - It helps you transition from block-based coding to text-based coding.
- ### How to Get Started:
  - Explore Blockly games at Blockly Games.

Ruby

- ### What Is Ruby?
  - Ruby is a language known for its simplicity and elegance.
- ### Why Try Ruby?
  - It's easy to read and write, making it great for beginners.
- ### How to Get Started:
  - Look for tutorials like Ruby for Kids.

Choosing the Right Language for You

You might be wondering which language to try next. Here's how you can decide:

- **Follow Your Interests:**
    - If you like making games, try Scratch or JavaScript.
    - If you're interested in robots or electronics, look into Python.
- **Ask for Advice:**
    - Talk to your parents, teachers, or friends who know about coding.
- **Try Them Out:**
    - Many languages have online platforms where you can try them without installing anything.

Tips for Continuing Your Coding Journey

Stay Curious

Always ask questions and explore new ideas.

- **Why does the code work this way?**
- **What happens if I change this part?**

Don't Be Afraid to Make Mistakes

Making mistakes is a big part of learning.

- **Learn from Errors:**
    - If your code doesn't work, that's okay! Try to figure out why and fix it.
- **Experiment:**
    - Try new things in your code to see what happens.

Seek Help When You Need It

Everyone needs help sometimes.

- **Ask Adults or Teachers:**
    - If you're stuck, ask someone with more experience.
- **Use Online Resources:**
    - There are many tutorials, forums, and videos that can help.

Keep It Fun!

Remember, coding should be enjoyable.

- **Work on Projects You Love:**
    - Choose projects that excite you.
- **Take Breaks:**
    -

If you get frustrated, take a short break and come back refreshed.

Final Thoughts

You've made incredible progress, and the coding world is full of endless possibilities. Whether you continue with Go or explore new languages, the most important thing is to keep learning and have fun.

Go the Gopher's Message to You

"Hey there, little coder! You've done an amazing job exploring the world of Go with me. Remember, coding is like a superpower—you can create anything you imagine. Keep practicing, keep exploring, and never stop having fun!"

Stay in Touch

- **Share Your Creations:**
  - We'd love to see what you build next!
- **Inspire Others:**
  - Teach your friends or siblings what you've learned.

Happy Coding!

Appendix

Glossary of Coding Terms

Welcome to the Glossary! Here, we'll explain some common coding words you've learned in this book. Understanding these terms will help you on your coding journey.

Algorithm

A set of step-by-step instructions to solve a problem or perform a task. It's like a recipe for cooking!

Array

A collection of items stored at neighboring memory locations. Think of it as a row of lockers, each holding a value.

Boolean

A data type that can be either true or false. It's like a light switch that's either on or off.

Bug

A mistake or error in a program that causes it to behave unexpectedly. Even the best programmers find bugs sometimes!

Code

Instructions written in a programming language that computers can understand.

Compiler

A tool that translates your code into a language the computer can run. It's like a translator between you and the computer.

Conditional Statement

A statement that runs code only if a certain condition is met, using if and else. It's how programs make decisions.

Data Type

The kind of data a variable can hold, like numbers (int), text (string), or true/false values (bool).

Debugging

The process of finding and fixing bugs in your code.

Function

A set of code that performs a specific task. It's like a mini-program within your program.

Loop

A way to repeat code multiple times. It's like telling the computer to do something over and over.

Parameter

A value you can pass to a function to customize it. It's like giving the function extra information.

Slice

A flexible collection of items, similar to an array but can grow or shrink in size.

String

A sequence of characters (letters, numbers, symbols) used to represent text.

Syntax

The set of rules that define how to write code in a programming language. It's like grammar for code.

Variable

A named space in memory where you can store data that can change. Think of it as a box with a label.

Helpful Resources for Kids

Keep learning and exploring with these fun and kid-friendly coding resources!

Websites

- **Go Playground**: An online place to write and run Go code without installing anything.
  - play.golang.org
- **Code.org**: Offers free coding lessons and games for kids of all ages.
  - code.org
- **Scratch**: A visual programming language where you can create stories, games, and animations.

- scratch.mit.edu
- **Blockly Games**: Learn programming concepts through games using visual blocks.
  - blockly.games

Books

- **"Hello World! Computer Programming for Kids and Other Beginners"** by Warren Sande and Carter Sande
- **"Python for Kids: A Playful Introduction to Programming"** by Jason R. Briggs
- **"Coding Games in Scratch"** by Jon Woodcock

Apps

- **Lightbot**: A puzzle game that introduces programming concepts.
- **Tynker**: Offers interactive courses and games to teach coding.
- **Kodable**: Teaches coding through engaging games for younger kids.

Coding Clubs and Programs

- **Girls Who Code**: Clubs and programs encouraging girls to pursue coding.

- o

    girlswhocode.com

- **CoderDojo**: Free programming clubs for young people.

    o

    coderdojo.com

- **Hour of Code**: One-hour tutorials introducing coding.

    o

    hourofcode.com

Videos and Tutorials

- **Code Monkey Island**: Fun videos teaching coding basics.
- **Go Programming Language YouTube Channel**: Official tutorials and talks about Go.

    o

    YouTube - Go

Answer Key to Exercises

Great job working through the exercises! Here are the answers to check your work.

Chapter 4: Numbers and Math Magic

Challenge 1: Birthday Countdown

go

package main

```go
import "fmt"
func main() {
    daysUntilBirthday := 10
    for i := daysUntilBirthday; i >= 1; i-- {
        fmt.Println("Only", i, "days until my birthday!")
    }
    fmt.Println("Happy Birthday to me! ")
}
```

Challenge 2: Animal Legs

go
```
package main
import "fmt"
func main() {
    cats := 3
    legsPerCat := 4
    totalLegs := cats * legsPerCat
    fmt.Println("Total legs:", totalLegs)
}
```

Challenge 3: Pocket Money

go

```go
package main

import "fmt"

func main() {
    startingMoney := 10
    toyCost := 4
    moneyLeft := startingMoney - toyCost
    fmt.Println("Money left:", moneyLeft)
}
```

Chapter 5: Storing Treasures: Variables

Challenge 1: Story Time

```go
package main

import "fmt"

func main() {
    characterName := "Lily"
    characterAge := 8
    favoriteHobby := "painting"
    fmt.Println("Once upon a time, there was a child named", characterName)
    fmt.Println("They were", characterAge, "years old and loved", favoriteHobby)
```

}

Challenge 2: Temperature Check

go

```
package main

import "fmt"

func main() {
    temperature := 25.5
    fmt.Println("Today's temperature is", temperature, "degrees Celsius.')
}
```

Challenge 3: Basketball Game

go

```
package main

import "fmt"

func main() {
    teamScore := 0
    fmt.Println("Team score:", teamScore)
    teamScore = teamScore + 2
    fmt.Println("Team scored a basket!")
    fmt.Println("Team score:", teamScore)
}
```

Chapter 6: Making Choices: If and Else

Challenge 1: Guess the Number Game

go

```go
package main

import "fmt"

func main() {
    var guess int
    secretNumber := 3
    fmt.Println("Guess the secret number between 1 and 5:")
    fmt.Scanln(&guess)
    if guess == secretNumber {
        fmt.Println("You guessed it!")
    } else {
        fmt.Println("Try again!")
    }
}
```

Challenge 2: Weather Suggestion

go

```go
package main

import "fmt"
```

```go
func main() {
    var weather string
    fmt.Println("What's the weather like today? ('sunny', 'rainy', 'snowy')")
    fmt.Scanln(&weather)
    if weather == "sunny" {
        fmt.Println("Great! Let's go to the park!")
    } else if weather == "rainy" {
        fmt.Println("Don't forget your umbrella!")
    } else if weather == "snowy" {
        fmt.Println("Time to build a snowman!")
    } else {
        fmt.Println(" Hmm, I don't recognize that weather.")
    }
}
```

Chapter 7: Loop-de-Loop: Doing Things Over and Over

Challenge 1: FizzBuzz Game

go

```
package main

import "fmt"
```

```go
func main() {
    for i := 1; i <= 15; i++ {
        if i%3 == 0 && i%5 == 0 {
            fmt.Println("FizzBuzz")
        } else if i%3 == 0 {
            fmt.Println("Fizz")
        } else if i%5 == 0 {
            fmt.Println("Buzz")
        } else {
            fmt.Println(i)
        }
    }
}
```

Challenge 2: Creating a Number Pyramid

```go
package main
import "fmt"
func main() {
    for i := 1; i <= 5; i++ {
        for j := 1; j <= i; j++ {
```

        fmt.Print(j, " ")
    }
    fmt.Println()
  }
}

Challenge 3: Custom Message Repeater

```go
package main

import "fmt"

func main() {
    var message string
    var times int
    fmt.Println("Enter a message:")
    fmt.Scanln(&message)
    fmt.Println("How many times do you want to repeat it?")
    fmt.Scanln(&times)
    for i := 1; i <= times; i++ {
        fmt.Println(message)
    }
}
```

Chapter 8: Fantastic Functions

Challenge 1: Calculating the Area of a Rectangle

```go
package main

import "fmt"

func calculateArea(length, width int) int {
    area := length * width
    return area
}

func main() {
    length := 6
    width := 4
    area := calculateArea(length, width)
    fmt.Println("The area of the rectangle is", area)
}
```

Challenge 2: Finding the Biggest Number

```go
package main

import "fmt"

func maxNumber(a, b int) int {
```

```go
    if a > b {
        return a
    } else {
        return b
    }
}

func main() {
    bigger := maxNumber(9, 12)
    fmt.Println("The bigger number is", bigger)
}
```

Challenge 3: Creating a Simple Calculator

```go
package main

import "fmt"

func add(a, b int) int {
    return a + b
}

func subtract(a, b int) int {
    return a - b
}
```

```go
func multiply(a, b int) int {
    return a * b
}
func divide(a, b int) int {
    return a / b
}
func main() {
    num1 := 20
    num2 := 4
    fmt.Println("Addition:", add(num1, num2))
    fmt.Println("Subtraction:", subtract(num1, num2))
    fmt.Println("Multiplication:", multiply(num1, num2))
    fmt.Println("Division:", divide(num1, num2))
}
```

Chapter 9: Collections of Fun: Arrays and Slices

Challenge 1: High Scores

go

```
package main
import "fmt"
func main() {
```

```go
    highScores := []int{}
    // Adding scores
    highScores = append(highScores, 100)
    highScores = append(highScores, 200)
    highScores = append(highScores, 150)
    fmt.Println("High Scores:")
    for _, score := range highScores {
        fmt.Println(score)
    }
}
```

Challenge 2: Favorite Colors

go

```
package main
import "fmt"
func main() {
    var colors []string
    var color string
    fmt.Println("Enter your favorite colors (type 'done' to finish):")
    for {
        fmt.Scanln(&color)
```

```go
    if color == "done" {
        break
    }
    colors = append(colors, color)
}
fmt.Println("Your favorite colors are:")
for _, c := range colors {
    fmt.Println("-", c)
}
}
```

Challenge 3: Animal List Sorting

```go
package main
import (
    "fmt"
    "sort"
)
func main() {
    animals := []string{"Zebra", "Elephant", "Lion", "Giraffe"}
    fmt.Println("Unsorted Animals:")
```

```go
    for _, animal := range animals {
        fmt.Println("-", animal)
    }
    // Sorting the slice
    sort.Strings(animals)
    fmt.Println("\nSorted Animals:")
    for _, animal := range animals {
        fmt.Println("-", animal)
    }
}
```

Chapter 10: Strings: Words and Sentences
Challenge 1: Word Guessing Game
go
```
package main

import (
    "fmt"
    "strings"
)

func main() {
    secretWord := "gopher"
```

```go
var guess string
fmt.Println("Guess the secret word:")
fmt.Scanln(&guess)
if strings.ToLower(guess) == secretWord {
    fmt.Println("You guessed it!")
} else {
    fmt.Println("Try again!")
}
}
```

Challenge 2: Pig Latin Translator

```go
package main
import "fmt"
func main() {
    word := "gopher"
    pigLatin := word[1:] + string(word[0]) + "ay"
    fmt.Println("Original word:", word)
    fmt.Println("Pig Latin:", pigLatin)
}
```

Challenge 3: Word Reverser

go

```go
package main

import (
    "fmt"
    "strings"
)

func main() {
    sentence := "Go is fun"
    words := strings.Split(sentence, " ")
    reversedWords := reverseWords(words)
    reversedSentence := strings.Join(reversedWords, " ")
    fmt.Println("Original:", sentence)
    fmt.Println("Reversed:", reversedSentence)
}

func reverseWords(words []string) []string {
    for i, j := 0, len(words)-1; i < j; i, j = i+1, j-1 {
        words[i], words[j] = words[j], words[i]
    }
    return words
}
```

Note: Some of the code examples require running on your computer because they use user input functions like fmt.Scanln, which may not work in online editors. Ask an adult to help you set up Go on your computer if you haven't already.

Congratulations!

You've reached the end of the book. Remember, coding is a journey filled with endless possibilities. Keep exploring, keep experimenting, and most importantly, have fun!

Happy Coding!